DISCOVERING
THE UNITED KINGDOM

ALL ABOUT
WALES

SUSAN HARRISON

BookLife

©2016
Book Life
King's Lynn
Norfolk PE30 4LS

ISBN: 978-1-910512-76-0

Written by:
Susan Harrison
Edited by:
Grace Jones
Designed by:
Drue Rintoul

A catalogue record for this book
is available from the British Library.

CONTENTS

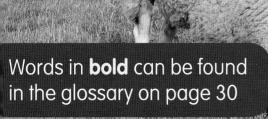

Words in **bold** can be found in the glossary on page 30

WELCOME TO WALES

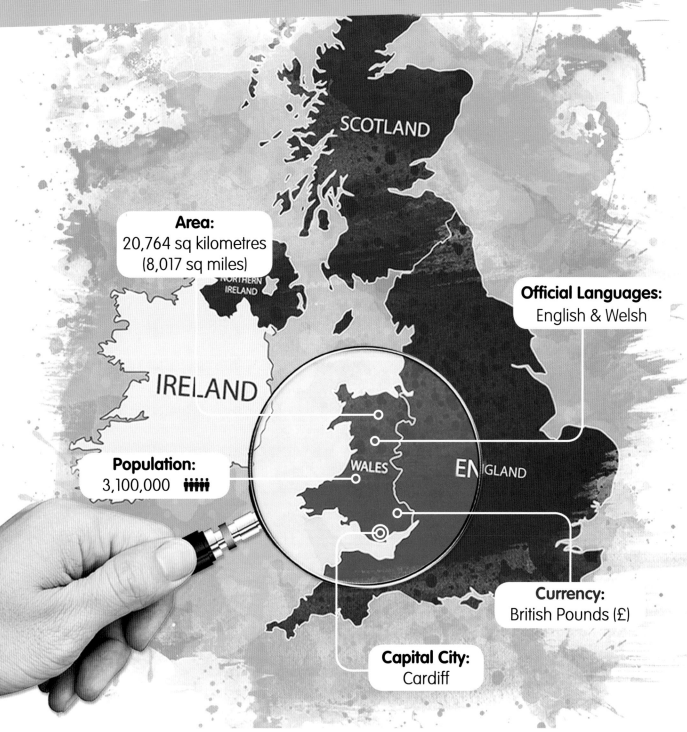

Area:
20,764 sq kilometres
(8,017 sq miles)

Official Languages:
English & Welsh

Population:
3,100,000

Currency:
British Pounds (£)

Capital City:
Cardiff

SCOTLAND

NORTHERN
IRELAND

IRELAND

WALES

ENGLAND

Wales is one of four countries which, together with **England**, **Scotland** and **Northern Ireland**, form the **United Kingdom**. It is in the South West of the UK, and is bordered by England.

Wales is made up of great mountain ranges, lush valleys and beautiful coastline as well as towns, cities and villages.

TAKE A LOOK www.visitwales.com/explore is a great website to look at to find out more about Wales.

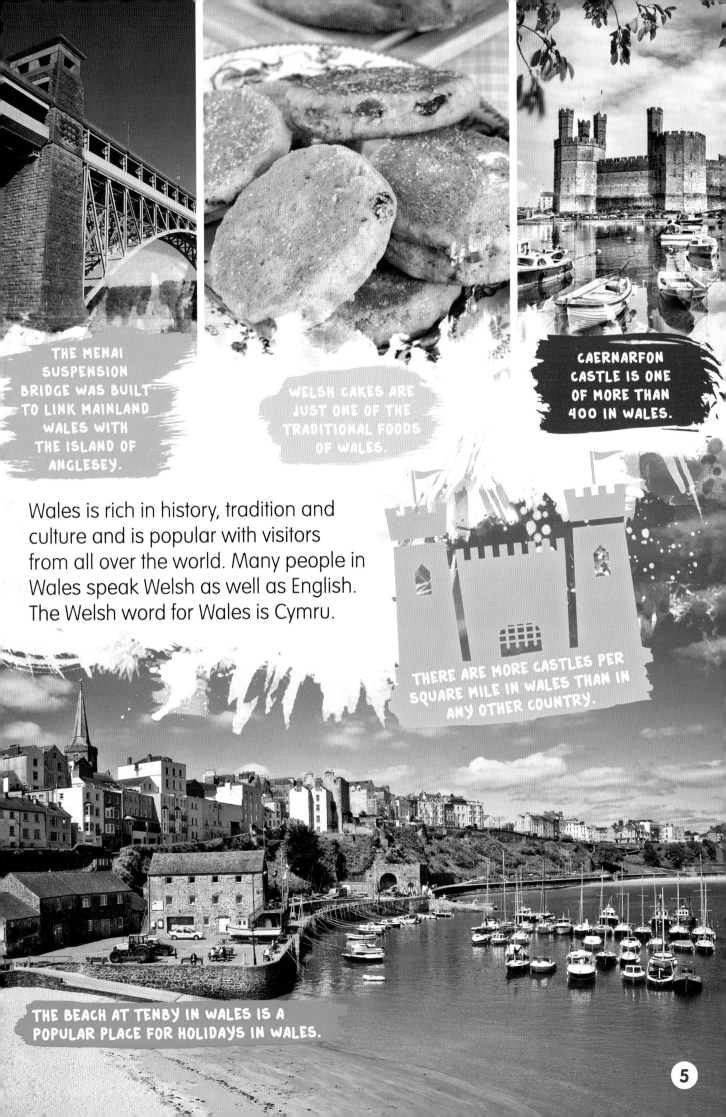

THE MENAI SUSPENSION BRIDGE WAS BUILT TO LINK MAINLAND WALES WITH THE ISLAND OF ANGLESEY.

WELSH CAKES ARE JUST ONE OF THE TRADITIONAL FOODS OF WALES.

CAERNARFON CASTLE IS ONE OF MORE THAN 400 IN WALES.

Wales is rich in history, tradition and culture and is popular with visitors from all over the world. Many people in Wales speak Welsh as well as English. The Welsh word for Wales is Cymru.

THERE ARE MORE CASTLES PER SQUARE MILE IN WALES THAN IN ANY OTHER COUNTRY.

THE BEACH AT TENBY IN WALES IS A POPULAR PLACE FOR HOLIDAYS IN WALES.

THE HISTORY OF WALES

Wales was inhabited by the Celts until the country was invaded by the Romans. When Anglo Saxons invaded from England, and the Vikings invaded from the sea, a number of different kingdoms were formed.

The Welsh kingdoms fought each other for power, but gradually Wales came under English control, and around 1283 King Edward I of England conquered the country.

THE OLDEST HUMAN REMAINS UNEARTHED IN WALES WERE FOUND IN THE VALLEY OF THE RIVER ELWY IN NORTH WALES, AND ARE BELIEVED TO BE 230,000 YEARS OLD.

THE RUINS OF FLINT CASTLE – THE FIRST CASTLE BUILT BY KING EDWARD I IN HIS BID TO CONQUER WALES.

BC 1000 – The Celts start to arrive in Wales

550 – The Saxons begin their advance on Wales

1283 – King Edward I orders the building of castles in Wales in a bid to conquer the country

48 – The Romans conquest of Wales begins

784 – Offa's Dyke is built by the King of Mercia to separate Wales from England

In 1536 the first Act of Union was passed between England and Wales. Wales was governed by English law. In 1999, after hundreds of years of English rule, the Welsh Assembly was established and Wales was given a government of its own. This is called the Welsh Assembly.

A CELTIC CROSS – A SYMBOL OF THE FIRST PEOPLE TO INHABIT WALES FROM AROUND BC1000.

1400 – Owain Glyndwr begins a Welsh revolt against the rule of King Henry IV

1955 – Cardiff is officially named the capital city of Wales

1284 – The Statute of Rhuddlan officially unites Wales under English Rule

1536 – An Act of Union is passed so that Wales will be governed by English law

1999 – The National Assembly for Wales is opened by Queen Elizabeth II

Wales is full of famous landmarks that help to tell the story of the history of the country as well as shaping the landscape. Some of them, such as The Wales Millennium Centre, the Menai Bridge, or the many castles, are manmade.

Many of Wales's landmarks are naturally occurring, and include the Snowdonia **National Park**, Three Cliff's Bay and the Pistyll Rhaeadr Waterfalls.

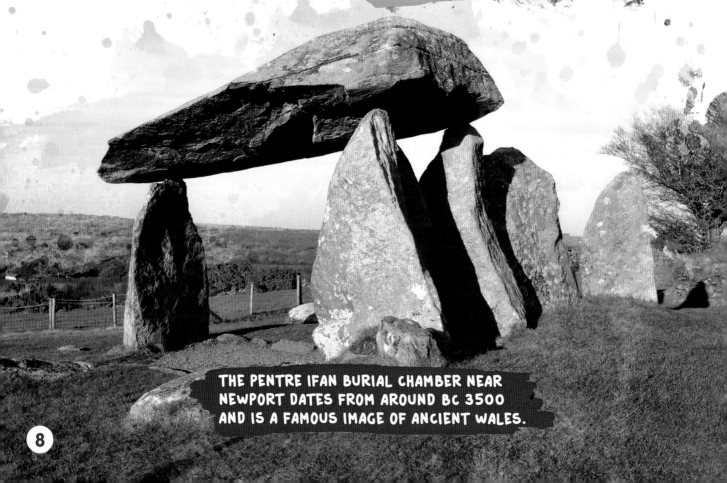

THE DEVIL'S BRIDGE FALLS NEAR ABERYSTWYTH ARE STEEPED IN LEGEND, AND ARE VISITED BY THOUSANDS OF TOURISTS EVERY YEAR.

THE PENTRE IFAN BURIAL CHAMBER NEAR NEWPORT DATES FROM AROUND BC 3500 AND IS A FAMOUS IMAGE OF ANCIENT WALES.

TAKE A LOOK To see more landmarks in Wales, take a look at
www.walesonline.co.uk/lifestyle/fun-stuff/how-many-welsh-landmarks-you-9200681

THE WORM'S HEAD IS A SMALL ISLAND NEAR RHOSSILI BAY. IT IS SHAPED LIKE A GIANT SEA-SERPENT AND IT TAKES ITS NAME FROM THE VIKING WORD 'WURM' WHICH MEANS 'DRAGON'.

Some of the most famous landmarks are also the most mysterious, with many legends and stories surrounding them.

THE MILLENNIUM STADIUM IN CARDIFF HAS THE LARGEST RETRACTABLE ROOF OF ANY SPORTS ARENA IN THE WORLD.

MOUNT SNOWDON IS THE TALLEST MOUNTAIN IN WALES, AT 1,085 METRES (3,560 FEET). MORE THAN 300,000 PEOPLE WALK TO THE SUMMIT OF MOUNT SNOWDON EVERY YEAR.

CLIMATE & LANDSCAPE

Wales is famous for being cloudy, wet and windy. It never gets too hot, or too cold, so the climate is described as temperate. June, July and August are usually the warmest months, and January is usually the coldest.

The middle of the country is full of hills, lakes and waterfalls. Wales also has a jagged coastline which is dotted with beaches.

PISTYLL RHAEADR IS A WATERFALL NEAR THE VILLAGE OF LLANRHAEADR-YM-MOCHNANT IN POWYS. IT IS HIGHER THAN NIAGARA FALLS, AND IS LISTED AS ONE OF THE SEVEN WONDERS OF WALES.

AT 886 METRES ABOVE SEA LEVEL, PEN Y FAN IS THE HIGHEST PEAK IN SOUTH WALES, SITUATED IN THE BRECON BEACONS NATIONAL PARK.

SNOWDONIA NATIONAL PARK HAS 9 MOUNTAIN RANGES, 90 PEAKS AND OVER 100 LAKES.

Snowdonia, the Pembrokeshire Coast and the Brecon Beacons are National Parks in Wales, and cover 4,143 square kilometres (1,599 square miles). They contain some of the most beautiful landscapes in the whole of the UK and are protected areas.

THERE ARE 15 MOUNTAINS IN WALES THAT HAVE A HEIGHT OF 3,000 FEET OR MORE (914.4 METRES).

LLYN TEGID IS ONE OF THE LARGEST BODIES OF WATER IN WALES. IT IS ALSO REPORTED TO BE ONE OF THE COLDEST. LEGEND HAS IT THAT, TEGGIE, IT'S VERY OWN SHY MONSTER, LURKS BENEATH THE SURFACE.

TOWNS & CITIES

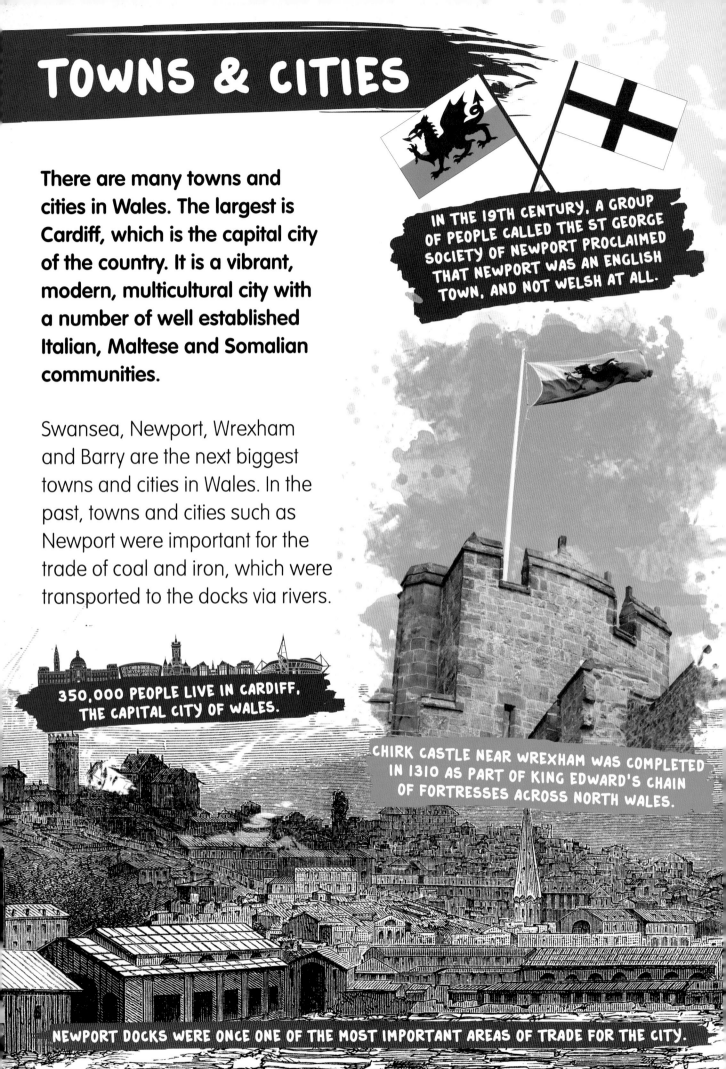

There are many towns and cities in Wales. The largest is Cardiff, which is the capital city of the country. It is a vibrant, modern, multicultural city with a number of well established Italian, Maltese and Somalian communities.

Swansea, Newport, Wrexham and Barry are the next biggest towns and cities in Wales. In the past, towns and cities such as Newport were important for the trade of coal and iron, which were transported to the docks via rivers.

IN THE 19TH CENTURY, A GROUP OF PEOPLE CALLED THE ST GEORGE SOCIETY OF NEWPORT PROCLAIMED THAT NEWPORT WAS AN ENGLISH TOWN, AND NOT WELSH AT ALL.

350,000 PEOPLE LIVE IN CARDIFF, THE CAPITAL CITY OF WALES.

CHIRK CASTLE NEAR WREXHAM WAS COMPLETED IN 1310 AS PART OF KING EDWARD'S CHAIN OF FORTRESSES ACROSS NORTH WALES.

NEWPORT DOCKS WERE ONCE ONE OF THE MOST IMPORTANT AREAS OF TRADE FOR THE CITY.

CREV·GWIR·IN·THESE·STONES
FEL·GWYDR·HORIZONS
OF·WRNAIS·AWEN·SING

THE MILLENNIUM CENTRE IN CARDIFF IS A FOCUS FOR ALL KINDS OF ARTS AND CULTURE.

The **economy** of Cardiff, like that of many cities, depends heavily on retail and **tourism**. Most people work in these sectors.

NEWPORT'S CATHEDRAL IS OFFICIALLY CALLED NEWPORT CATHEDRAL OF ST WOOLOS, KING & CONFESSOR

THE COUNTRYSIDE & WILDLIFE

The Welsh countryside is full of natural beauty, and is very important for wildlife. Thousands of different species of plants, flowers, birds and animals live there in the hills and the valleys, and along the coastline.

Some rare species of plants, such as the Snowdon Lily, Yellow Whitlow Grass and Wild Asparagus grow in Wales. It is the only place in the UK where they can be found.

THE BRECON BEACONS ARE HOME TO SOME OF THE PRETTIEST BREEDS OF MOUNTAIN PONIES.

THE ISLANDS OF SKOKHOLM AND SKOMER, JUST OFF THE COAST OF SOUTH WALES, ARE HOME TO MORE THAN HALF THE WORLD'S POPULATION OF MANX SHEARWATERS.

POTATOES ARE A COMMON AGRICULTURAL CROP IN WALES.

Because there is a lot of poor quality soil in the hilly landscapes of Wales, much of the countryside is unsuitable for crops. Livestock **farming** is more common and Wales is especially famous for sheep farming.

THERE ARE MORE THAN 11 MILLION SHEEP IN WALES.

MONTGOMERYSHIRE WILDLIFE TRUST HAS NINE SITES, DESIGNED TO ENCOURAGE THE PEARL BORDERED FRITILLARY BUTTERFLY TO BREED AND TO STOP IT BECOMING EXTINCT.

MUCH OF WALES IS UNSUITABLE FOR CROP-GROWING, SO LIVESTOCK FARMING IS MORE COMMON.

THE COASTLINE

Wales has a striking, jagged coastline with a huge variety of marine life. The coastline attracts thousands of visitors every year, with many visiting the seaside towns such as Llandudno or Tenby for family holidays. Others enjoy the long walks along the interesting coastline.

There are also more than 60 islands off the coast of Wales. The largest of these is Anglesey, which is linked to the mainland by the Menai Bridge.

IN 2012, THE WALES COASTAL PATH WAS OPENED. IT IS THE WORLD'S FIRST CLEAR PATH ALONG A NATIONAL COAST.

WALES HAS 1208 KILOMETRES (750 MILES) OF COASTLINE.

SEA FISHING IS A DECLINING INDUSTRY IN WALES, BUT IS STILL IMPORTANT TO MANY PEOPLE WHO LIVE AND WORK ALONG THE COAST.

THE UK'S BIGGEST POD OF DOLPHINS LIVES IN CARDIGAN BAY AND REGULARLY SHOWS OFF FOR VISITORS.

These islands are home to many different species of wildlife, ranging from rare birds to seals.

SKOMER ISLAND IS FAMOUS FOR THE HUGE NUMBERS OF PUFFINS THAT LIVE THERE.

17

PEOPLE

The Welsh people are very proud of their heritage. All children have to learn to speak Welsh in school until they are 16.

Most people who live in Welsh towns and cities live in modern brick houses, blocks of flats or old terraced houses. In the countryside there are lots of pretty cottages.

CHILDREN IN WALES START SCHOOL WHEN THEY ARE FIVE.

ABOUT A FIFTH OF SCHOOLS IN WALES TEACH CHILDREN ALL THEIR SUBJECTS IN WELSH.

THE LEEK AND THE DAFFODIL ARE BOTH NATIONAL EMBLEMS OF WALES.

SOME PEOPLE IN THE COUNTRYSIDE LIVE IN PRETTY STONE COTTAGES.

WELCOME TO WALES	CROESO I GYMRU
GOOD MORNING	BORE DA
MY NAME IS	YDW I
HOW ARE YOU?	SUT MAE?
MY HEAD HURTS	MAE PEN TOST GYDA FI

MOST PEOPLE IN WALES LIVE AND WORK IN TOWNS AND CITIES.

Christianity is the largest religion in Wales, with many Catholic and Baptist churches. Many other faiths are practised in the country as it becomes an increasingly multicultural society, particularly in towns and cities.

Ydych chi wedi talu ac arddangos?

Have you paid and displayed?

OVER HALF A MILLION PEOPLE IN WALES SPEAK WELSH AS THEIR FIRST LANGUAGE.

ONLY 10% OF THE WELSH POPULATION GOES TO CHURCH.

CULTURE, LEISURE AND TOURISM

Wales is well known for being a place full of culture, with a history of producing great writers, artists and musicians. There are also lots of historically important places to visit, where you can learn more about the history of the country.

Writers such as Roald Dahl and C.S. Lewis have strong family links to Wales. Dylan Thomas is probably the country's most famous writer. Many people visit Wales to find out more about him.

The Enormous Crocodile
by Roald Dahl
Illustrated by Quentin Blake

FAMOUS TV PROGRAMMES DR WHO AND TORCHWOOD ARE FILMED IN CARDIFF.

FAMOUS AUTHOR ROALD DAHL WAS BORN IN CARDIFF – THOUGH HIS PARENTS WERE NORWEGIAN.

THE WALES MILLENNIUM CENTRE IS THE MOST VISITED TOURIST ATTRACTION IN WALES.

PEOPLE COME FROM ALL OVER THE WORLD TO VISIT THE OLD BOATHOUSE WHERE AUTHOR DYLAN THOMAS USED TO LIVE AND WORK. HIS MOST FAMOUS BOOK IS UNDER MILKWOOD.

People from all over the world visit Wales to find out more about the culture, visiting the museums, castles and **festivals**.

SPORT

THE MILLENNIUM STADIUM CAN HOLD 74,500 PEOPLE.

The most popular sports in Wales are rugby and football. The Millennium Stadium in Cardiff is the country's national stadium.

THE MILLENNIUM STADIUM IN CARDIFF WAS HOME TO THE ENGLAND FOOTBALL AND RUGBY TEAMS WHILE THEY WAITED A VERY LONG TIME FOR THE NEW WEMBLEY STADIUM TO BE BUILT!

The country has produced many famous sportsmen, including footballer Ryan Giggs, cyclist Geraint Thomas, golfer Ian Woosnam, athlete Colin Jackson and rugby players such as Scott Quinell and Gareth Edwards. A record number of Welsh athletes were included in Team GB for the 2012 Olympic Games.

WALES HAS WON THE SIX NATIONS RUGBY CHAMPIONSHIP 26 TIMES.

RUGBY IS ONE OF THE MOST POPULAR SPORTS IN WALES, WITH MILLIONS OF FANS SUPPORTING LOCAL AND NATIONAL TEAMS.

TAKE A LOOK For more information about sport in Wales visit, **www.sport.wales**

WELSH ATHLETE COLIN JACKSON HELD THE WORLD RECORD FOR 110M HURDLES AT 12.91 SECONDS FOR MORE THAN A DECADE.

Welsh people are passionate about sport, and participate in lots of outdoor activities, enjoying the stunning mountains, valleys, rivers and coastlines of the country.

THE RYDER CUP GOLF CHAMPIONSHIP WAS HELD IN NEWPORT, SOUTH WALES IN 2010.

THE LANDSCAPE OF WALES MAKES OUTDOOR SPORTS SUCH AS CLIMBING, SWIMMING, MOUNTAIN BIKING AND HIKING POPULAR WITH WELSH PEOPLE.

TRADITIONS

Wales is a country full of traditions and national pride. The Welsh people enjoy many festivals and events throughout the year, to celebrate their customs and history.

Wales is often called 'the land of song' and is well known for its famous choirs, harpists and solo singers. This musical heritage is celebrated with a special competition called the National Eisteddfod, where people come together to compete in singing, music and literature.

ST DAVID IS THE PATRON SAINT OF WALES. HE IS CELEBRATED ON ST DAVID'S DAY ON MARCH 1ST EVERY YEAR.

IN 1797, FRENCH TROOPS LANDED IN LLANWNDA. AFTER DRINKING A LITTLE BIT TOO MUCH SO THEY WERE UNABLE TO FIGHT, THEY SPOTTED WHAT THEY THOUGHT WERE THOUSANDS OF ENGLISH MILITIA, AND SURRENDERED. IN FACT, THERE WERE ONLY A FEW MILITIA MEN AROUND AT THE TIME. WHAT THEY HAD SEEN WAS LOTS OF WOMEN DRESSED IN TRADITIONAL WELSH COSTUME!

MARI LWYD IS AN OLD TRADITION THAT INVOLVES PUTTING A FAKE HORSE'S HEAD ON A POLE, AND CHALLENGING YOUR NEIGHBOURS TO A BATTLE OF RHYMING WELSH INSULTS.

NO FESTIVAL OR CELEBRATION WOULD BE COMPLETE WITHOUT TRADITIONAL WELSH CAKES.

THE WELSH NATIONAL ANTHEM WAS WRITTEN IN 1856 BY EVAN JAMES AND HIS SON.

The land of my fathers,
the land of my choice,
The land in which poets
and minstrels rejoice;
The land whose stern warriors
were true to the core,
While bleeding from freedom
of yore.

Food and drink feature heavily in many Welsh festivals, and favourite recipes such as Welsh Cakes, Bara Brith and Cawl are important in the celebrations.

THE TRADITIONAL WELSH DISH OF CAWL IS MADE FROM DIFFERENT INGREDIENTS DEPENDING ON WHERE YOU ARE IN THE COUNTRY.

QUICK QUIZ

Have you been paying attention? Let's find out!
Take our quick quiz to see how much you have found out in this book.

1. WHAT IS THE POPULATION OF WALES?

2. HOW MANY MILES OF COASTLINE DOES WALES HAVE?

3. WHAT IS THE NAME OF THE CAPITAL CITY OF WALES?

4. WHAT IS THE LAND AREA OF WALES?

5. WHO BUILT FLINT CASTLE?

6. WHAT IS THE NAME OF THE TALLEST MOUNTAIN IN WALES?

7. WHERE IS CHIRK CASTLE?

8. WHAT DOES THE VIKING WORD 'WURM' MEAN?

9. WHAT IS THE NAME OF THE HIGHEST WATERFALL IN WALES?

10. HOW MANY MOUNTAINS IN WALES ARE TALLER THAN 3,000FT?

11. HOW MANY PEOPLE LIVE IN CARDIFF?

12. WHAT IS THE OFFICIAL NAME OF NEWPORT'S CATHEDRAL?

13. HOW MANY SHEEP ARE THERE IN WALES?

14. HOW MANY KILOMETRES OF COASTLINE DOES WALES HAVE?

15. WHERE IN WALES WOULD YOU FIND PUFFINS?

16. WHAT IS WELSH FOR 'GOOD MORNING'?

17. WHO IS THE PATRON SAINT OF WALES?

18. WHERE WAS ROALD DAHL BORN?

19. WHAT YEAR WAS THE RYDER CUP HELD IN WALES?

20. WHO WROTE THE WELSH NATIONAL ANTHEM?

USEFUL LINKS

Useful websites to help you find out more about Wales

WWW.WALES.COM

WWW.BBC.CO.UK/WALES/HISTORY

WWW.VISITWALES.COM

WWW.WALESONLINE.CO.UK

WWW.NATIONALTRUST.ORG.UK/VISIT/WALES

WWW.WTWALES.ORG

WWW.SPORT.WALES

WWW.CASTLEWALES.COM

PLACES TO VISIT

Interesting places to visit in Wales

SNOWDONIA
www.SNOWDONIATOURISM.CO.UK

NATIONAL MUSEUM OF WALES
www.MUSEUMWALES.AC.UK

THE MILLENNIUM CENTRE
www.WMC.ORG.UK

ST FAGAN'S NATURAL HISTORY MUSEUM
www.MUSEUMWALES.AC.UK/STFAGANS

THE NATIONAL WATERFRONT MUSEUM
www.MUSEUMWALES.AC.UK/SWANSEA

THE NATIONAL ROMAN LEGION MUSEUM
www.MUSEUMWALES.AC.UK/ROMAN/ABOUT

OFFA'S DYKE
www.NATIONALTRAIL.CO.UK/OFFAS-DYKE-PATH

THE NATIONAL WOOL MUSEUM
www.MUSEUMWALES.AC.UK/WOOL

THE HAY FESTIVAL
www.HAYFESTIVAL.COM

THE NATIONAL EISTEDDFOD
www.EISTEDDFOD.ORG.UK/ENGLISH

THE MILLENNIUM STADIUM
www.MILLENNIUMSTADIUM.COM

CAERNARFON CASTLE
www.CAERNARFON-CASTLE.CO.UK

THE NATIONAL SHOWCAVES CENTRE
www.SHOWCAVES.CO.UK

THE ISLAND OF ANGLESEY
www.VISITANGLESEY.CO.UK

GLOSSARY

CLIMATE	weather conditions
CULTURE	a way of life and traditions of a group of people
CURRENCY	the money a country uses
ECONOMY	the way trade and money are controlled by a country
FESTIVALS	occasions where people celebrate and enjoy culture
FARMING	growing or raising either crops or animals
LANDMARKS	places or buildings that are easily recognised
LANDSCAPES	physical features such as mountains, rivers, hills or coastlines
LEISURE	what people do in their spare time
NATIONAL PARKS	undeveloped areas of land looked after and protected for visitors to enjoy
TOURISM	attracting visitors from other places

Photocredits: Abbreviations: l-left, r-right, b-bottom, t-top, c-centre, m-middle, bg–background. All images are courtesy of Shutterstock.com.
Front Cover: t – Samot, ml – Oliver Hoffmann, mr – David Hughes, bl – Becky Stares, br – stocker1970, 3 – Diego Barbieri, 3 – 1000 Words, 4bg – okili77, 4front – tanatat, 5tl – Gail Johnson, 5tc – D. Pimborough, 5tr – Samot, 5b – Michael Hathway, 6/7 – Bahadir Yeniceri, 7tl – Jakkrit Orrasri, 7tr – Jakkrit Orrasri, 8t – DaBe86, 8b – StuartH, 9t – ian woolcock, 9m – M Mohammed, 9b – ian woolcock, 10t – Steve Allen, 10b – Mel Manser Photography, 11t – Gail Johnson, 11b – ian woolcock, 12m – Stephen Meese, 12/13 – Morphart Creation, 13t – Gail Johnson, 14t – marilyn barbone, 14b – krisgillam, 15t – rangizzz, 15m – MarkMirror, 15b – Simon Baylis, 16t – Mike Charles, 16b – mubus7, 17t – gfdunt, 17m – Elena Larina, 17b – Michael Thaler, 18t – racorn, 18m – marilyn barbone, 18b – Radek Sturgolewski, 19t – Visanuyotin, 19b – Lian Deng, 19inset – northallertonman, 20t – Graeme Dawes, 20m – Neftali, 20/21 – Shaun Jeffers, 21 – BasPhoto, 22t – Deymos.HR, 22m – MA PHOTOGRAPY, 22b – marcokenya, 23tl – Featureflash, 23tr – bikeriderlondon, 23m – Warren Goldswain, 23b – Lee Billinghurst, 24t – Alistair Scott, 24bl – Marzolino, 24br – jayteel, 25tl – neil langan, 25tr – stockphoto-graf, 25b – Fanfo,